#AtEaseJournal

to ....

from ....

date ....

Use the scriptures in this book for daily devotion.
Prayers and reflections go in the blank pages.
Then, spend time in prayer. Tell God about
the areas in life where you need relief.
Trust that He's listening. Know that He cares.

"At Ease, Soldier"

I AM NEVER ALONE BECAUSE GOD IS ALWAYS WITH ME.

Deuteronomy 31:6

AT EASE – Take it to God in Prayer

FEAR HAS NO HOLD ON ME BECAUSE GOD HAS GIVEN ME A SPIRIT OF POWER, LOVE, AND A SOUND MIND.

2 Timothy 1:7

AT EASE – Take it to God in Prayer

GOD'S TIMING IS ALWAYS RIGHT, AND I WILL WAIT PATIENTLY.

Psalm 27:14

AT EASE – Take it to God in Prayer

I AM MORE THAN A CONQUEROR THROUGH CHRIST.

Romans 8:37

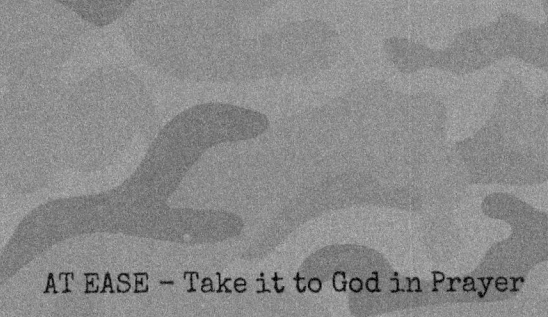

AT EASE – Take it to God in Prayer

I CHOOSE FAITH OVER FEAR AND JOY OVER STRESS.

Philippians 4:6-7

AT EASE – Take it to God in Prayer

I FORGIVE OTHERS AS CHRIST HAS FORGIVEN ME.

Ephesians 4:32

AT EASE – Take it to God in Prayer

MY BODY IS A TEMPLE OF THE HOLY SPIRIT, AND I HONOR IT.

1 Corinthians 6:19-20

AT EASE - Take it to God in Prayer

I CAN DO ALL THINGS THROUGH CHRIST WHO STRENGTHENS ME.

Philippians 4:13

AT EASE - Take it to God in Prayer

I LET GO OF ANXIETY AND EMBRACE GOD'S PEACE.

1 Peter 5:7

AT EASE – Take it to God in Prayer

I RECEIVE GOD'S WISDOM AND GUIDANCE IN ALL DECISIONS.

James 1:5

AT EASE – Take it to God in Prayer

I WALK BY FAITH, NOT BY SIGHT.

2 Corinthians 5:7

AT EASE – Take it to God in Prayer

I TRUST THAT GOD HAS A PERFECT PLAN FOR MY LIFE.

Jeremiah 29:11

AT EASE – Take it to God in Prayer

THE LORD IS MY SHEPHERD; I LACK NOTHING.

Psalm 23:1

AT EASE – Today with God in Prayer

I HAVE THE PEACE OF GOD THAT SURPASSES ALL UNDERSTANDING.

Philippians 4:7

AT EASE – Take it to God in Prayer

I RELEASE MY WORRIES AND TRUST IN GOD'S PROVISION.

Matthew 6:25-26

AT EASE – Take it to God in Prayer

**I AM SAFE
AND PROTECTED
UNDER GOD'S
MIGHTY HAND.**

Psalm 91:1-2

AT EASE – Take it to God in Prayer

I AM AT PEACE, KNOWING GOD IS IN CONTROL.

Isaiah 26:3

AT EASE – Take it to God in Prayer

I AM STRONG AND COURAGEOUS BECAUSE GOD GOES BEFORE ME.

Deuteronomy 31:8

AT EASE - Take it to God in Prayer

I WILL NOT BE SHAKEN, FOR GOD IS MY ROCK AND REFUGE.

Psalm 62:6

AT EASE - Take it to God in Prayer

GOD HAS EQUIPPED ME FOR EVERY GOOD WORK.

2 Timothy 3:17

AT EASE – Take it to God in Prayer

GOD'S MERCY IS NEW EVERY MORNING, AND I EMBRACE IT.

Lamentations 3:22-23

AT EASE – Take it to God in Prayer

MY HEART IS FILLED WITH JOY, REGARDLESS OF CIRCUMSTANCES.

Habakkuk 3:17-18

AT EASE – Take it to God in Prayer

GOD IS WORKING ALL THINGS TOGETHER FOR MY GOOD.

Romans 8:28

AT EASE – Take it to God in Prayer

MY GIFTS
AND TALENTS
ARE MEANT
TO BLESS OTHERS.

1 Peter 4:10

AT EASE – Take it to God in Prayer

**GOD IS
RENEWING MY MIND
DAILY
WITH HIS TRUTH.**

Romans 12:2

AT EASE − Take it to God in Prayer

I AM A LIGHT IN THIS WORLD, SHINING FOR GOD'S GLORY.

Matthew 5:14-16

AT EASE – Take it to God in Prayer

GOD IS DIRECTING MY STEPS TOWARD MY DESTINY.

Proverbs 16:9

AT EASE – Take it to God in Prayer

GOD'S LOVE FOR ME IS UNSHAKABLE AND UNCONDITIONAL.

Romans 8:38-39

AT EASE – Take it to God in Prayer

GOD'S GRACE IS SUFFICIENT FOR ME IN ALL SITUATIONS.

2 Corinthians 12:9

AT EASE - Take it to God in Prayer

MY LIFE IS A TESTIMONY OF GOD'S GOODNESS.

Psalm 40:2-3

AT EASE – Take it to God in Prayer

I AM VICTORIOUS IN CHRIST, AND NOTHING CAN SEPARATE ME FROM HIS LOVE.

1 Corinthians 15:57 / Romans 8:37-39

AT EASE – Take it to God in Prayer

GOD IS RESTORING EVERYTHING THE ENEMY HAS TRIED TO STEAL FROM ME.

Joel 2:25

AT EASE – Take it to God in Prayer

I AM FULFILLING GOD'S PURPOSE FOR MY LIFE.

Philippians 2:13 / Ephesians 2:10

AT EASE – Take it to God in Prayer

I REST IN THE PRESENCE OF GOD AND FIND PEACE.

Matthew 11:28-29

AT EASE – Take it to God in Prayer

GOD'S LOVE FILLS ME WITH UNSHAKABLE PEACE.

John 14:27

AT EASE – Take it to God in Prayer

I AM GRATEFUL FOR EVERY BLESSING GOD HAS GIVEN ME.

1 Thessalonians 5:18

AT EASE – Take it to God in Prayer

I AM CONTENT IN EVERY SEASON OF LIFE, KNOWING GOD IS WITH ME.

Philippians 4:11-12

AT EASE – Take it to God in Prayer

I AM FREE FROM GUILT AND SHAME BECAUSE JESUS HAS REDEEMED ME.

Romans 8:1-2

AT EASE – Take it to God in Prayer

GOD'S POWER IS MADE PERFECT IN MY WEAKNESS.

2 Corinthians 12:9

AT EASE – Take it to God in Prayer

THE JOY OF THE LORD IS MY STRENGTH.

Nehemiah 8:10

AT EASE – Take it to God in Prayer

I AM A VESSEL OF GOD'S LOVE AND KINDNESS.

Ephesians 2:10

AT EASE – Take it to God in Prayer

I AM FEARLESS BECAUSE GOD FIGHTS MY BATTLES.

Exodus 14:14

AT EASE – Take it to God in Prayer

NO WEAPON FORMED AGAINST ME SHALL PROSPER.

Isaiah 54:17

AT EASE – Take it to God in Prayer

GOD'S ANGELS SURROUND AND PROTECT ME WHEREVER I GO.

Psalm 91:11-12

AT EASE – Take it to God in Prayer

BY HIS STRIPES, I AM HEALED.

Isaiah 53:5

AT EASE – Take it to God in Prayer

I AM CREATED FOR GOD'S PURPOSE.

Ephesians 2:10

AT EASE – Take it to God in Prayer

I AM ANOINTED AND CHOSEN BY GOD.

1 Peter 2:9

AT EASE – Take it to God in Prayer

**MY PAST
DOES NOT DEFINE ME;
I AM A NEW CREATION
IN CHRIST.**

2 Corinthians 5:17

AT EASE – Take it to God in Prayer

I WALK BOLDLY IN THE CALLING GOD HAS GIVEN ME.

Joshua 1:9

AT EASE – Take it to God in Prayer

WORRY HAS NO PLACE IN MY HEART BECAUSE I TRUST IN GOD.

Matthew 6:34

AT EASE – Take it to God in Prayer

www.ingramcontent.com/pod-product-compliance
Lightning Source LLC
Chambersburg PA
CBHW061811070526
44586CB00024B/2809